I0160126

Anonymous

True Spiritualism

Anonymous

True Spiritualism

ISBN/EAN: 9783337341473

Printed in Europe, USA, Canada, Australia, Japan

Cover: Foto ©Lupo / pixelio.de

More available books at **www.hansebooks.com**

BY

Normon Leander.

———◇———

PHILADELPHIA :
KING & BAIRD, PRINTERS, 607 SANSOM STREET.
1875.

Entered according to Act of Congress in the year 1875, by

NORMON LEANDER,

In the Office of the Librarian of Congress at Washington.

PREFACE.

"What is spiritualism?" is a question that has been asked of late by those who never before gave any attention to the subject. The following pages will partially answer that question.

Recent occurrences involving the genuiness of certain spirit manifestations, which obtained great publicity, it was supposed by many, would throw a doubt on the public mind upon the truthfulness of the whole subject of spiritualism, but such is not the case. A spirit of inquiry has been awakened to an extent never before known.

Truth never suffers, its march is onward, its force irresistible. Error,

fraud, fanaticism and credulity, at times
may appear to overwhelm it, but the
apparent triumph will be of short duration, the latter must perish.

The statement headed " True Spiritualism," is supposed to embrace the general
principles. The several chapters containing brief explanations, are more particularly designed to call the attention of
the honest inquirer to the beautiful truths
contained therein, leaving him to form
his own conclusions.

In arranging the matter for publication,
the author, of course, consulted the lead-
ing works on Spiritualism, and made such
extracts from them as he deemed necessary to fairly place the subject before the
reader.

Valuable aid was derived from that
excellent book " The Problem of Life

and Immorality," by Loring Moody,
and from "Spiritualism," by Edmunds
and Dexter, with other standard works.

The true spiritualists have no sympa-
thy with modern manifestations, or with
the principles and practice of certain
parties who have assumed the name.

A large number of persons who have
made the subject of spirit manifestations, in all their different phrases, a
study for years, are not prepared to
believe in the truthfulness of SPIRIT
MATERIALIZATION. To them no satisfactory
evidence of its genuineness has yet ap-
peared. Great difference of opinion
exists on the subject among honest in-
vestigators. The reader will remember
that spiritualists are not responsible for
the articles contained in the newspapers,
supposed to be the organs of the be-

lievers in the Harmonial Philosophy. The publishers chronicle the current events of the day, leaving it to their readers to judge of their merits, and are not supposed to endorse everything that appears in their papers.

The genuine Spiritualist has more regard for truth than public opinion, and

"In strong integrity of soul
    Uplifted calmly stands, and hears the words
    Of stormy folly breaking at his feet."

No change of time or circumstances will ever alter his faith in what God in nature and his own judgment teaches him to be true. For these teachings and their author he has "a high sense of conscientiousness and a deep and solemn veneration."

THE AUTHOR.

PHILADELPHIA, *February* 20, 1875.

TRUE SPIRITUALISM.

First. That there is one vast sea of life, emanating from the Great First Cause, the Divine Mind, the Great Spirit.

Second. That forms of matter are the result of the operation of natural laws, unseen vital force, invisible powers, operating in this sea of life, under the guidance of Infinite Wisdom, for a purpose.

Third. That these forms of matter, from the lowest to the highest, came into existence in accordance with the laws of necessity in the Divine plan.

Fourth. The great centre of all things being spiritual, all power is necessarily spiritual.

Fifth. That man being the highest order of organized intelligence, has a spiritual nature as well as a corporeal; the spiritual having an organized form, with parts and organs corresponding to those of the visible body.

Sixth. That the body being but matter, is formed as a covering for the spirit by the operation of natural law, in accordance with the requirements and necessities of each individual for a use, serve its purpose, and then by the operation of the same law, disintegrate and fade away. The living organized spiritual being remains and is immortal, having continued identity, mental and moral growth.

Seventh. That there is a spiritual world, a place of existence for man after he has become separated from the external form, with its substantial realities adapted to the wants and necessities of his continued existence. That the change called physical death, a separation of matter and spirit, is a necessity of his nature quite as much as birth, and does not essentially change the mental condition or other characteristics of any when experienced.

Eighth. That after the process of physical death, the condition of man in the spirit world depends not upon arbitrary decree or special provision made by a superior, but on character, aspirations and personal individual conformity, to the universal divine law of his nature.

Ninth. That growth and development is the law of the human being, and is the endless progressive destiny of all.

Tenth. That as individuals are continually passing from the earthly to the spirit world in all stages and conditions of mental and moral growth, the spirit world necessarily includes all grades of character, from the lowest to the highest.

Eleventh. That happiness and misery depend on the growth and development of moral purity, and there must be as many grades of each in the spirit-world as there are shades of character, each gravitating to its own place by the natural law of affinity.

Twelfth. That through the law of spiritual affinity, there may be, and, doubtless are, by mental impression or other modes of transmission, communications, to a limited extent, from spirits out of the form, to spirits in the form ; but these communications are to be regarded as truths, just as communications from one person to another while on earth. Their character for truthfulness depends entirely upon the mental and moral development of both—the one that gives and the one that receives.

Thirteenth. That these communications or influx of ideas and promptings from the spirit world are not to be regarded as special privileges, confined to one class of persons, but have existed and will exist through all time and among all classes of persons ; they are the operation of natural law.

Fourteenth. That the chain of causation traced backward from what we see in nature leads inevitably to a Great First Cause, the fountain of life, love and wisdom, the source of all power, sustaining to all individualized intelligence, the relation of *father*, consequently all are *brethren*.

Fifteenth. That man as the offspring of the Divine has within him a germ of divinity, which is ever prompting him toward perfection, and that all evil in man is a want of harmony with this Divine principle, caused by an undeveloped mental and moral condition.

Sixteenth. That growth in goodness and truth is slow, depending, to some extent on physical organization and surrounding circumstances, but mainly upon interior growth; the ultimate destiny of all is perfection and happiness.

Seventeenth. Man's highest duty in this world is to assist in the mental and spiritual development of his kind, for such is the fundamental unity of human interests. So completely are our essential lives merged into each other, that the highest good and happiness of each individual can only be obtained through the highest good and happiness of all.

Eighteenth. The sufferings of this life are the necessary results of man's structure, are essential conditions of his mental, moral and spiritual culture and development; they are part of the divine economy, and the only methods by which we can ever reach high attainments and beneficent results. No man can appreciate spiritual refinement and exaltation, or comprehend the full measure of happiness and joy, until he has felt the sharp pangs of suffering and woe.

Nineteenth. That in proportion to man's *moral purity* will be his happiness, here and hereafter.

CHAPTER I.

First. That there is one vast sea of life, emanating from the Great First Cause, the Divine Mind, the Great Spirit.

Second. That forms of matter are the result of the operation of natural laws, unseen vital force, invisible powers operating in this sea of life, under the guidance of Infinite Wisdom, for a purpose.

Third. That these forms of matter, from the lowest to the highest, came into existence in accordance with the laws of necessity in the Divine plan.

The human mind when perfectly formed, is so constructed, that it cannot depart from the idea of a FIRST CAUSE possessing *All Power.* The source of all intelligence. A DEITY. A GREAT SPIRIT.

When there is real or apparent departure from this natural idea, it is only in proportion to the imperfection of the mental organization.

Different nations have names for this Great Spirit, corresponding to their degree of mental and moral development. Capacity to understand spiritual truths. ALLAH, JEHOVAH, GOD, &c., each name having a signification, embracing the peculiar idea they entertain of Him.

All nations use the masculine gender, growing

out of the notion of *strength* and *greatness*. We will do the same, and use the commonly received name—GOD.

Each person's conception of God, depends on the organization of the mind, the nature and character of the education, the degree of mental and moral development, and from this fact there must necessarily be great diversity of opinion as to His character and attributes.

To the mind, however, unbiassed by early education or sectarian influence, capable of comprehending truth, however and wherever it may be found, GOD is regarded as a GREAT SELF-EXISTING FACT, a REALITY, a GRAND CENTRE, a *Living Eternal Principal*, possessing all power and intelligence, manifesting His will and pleasure by the operation of fixed laws, producing the different forms of matter in nature, organizing, individualizing life and mind, and imparting to each, necessary intelligence, according to a pre-determined plan, for a purpose. Absolute and perfect in consequence and results.

These laws which we for convenience sake divide into Mechanical, Chemical, Electrical—laws of attraction and repulsion, centripetal and centrifugal forces, with the generative and organic processes and operations, by which spirit, mind and matter become associated, and

are brought to conscious individualized existence, are but the emanations of His power and
will, vital forces, natural laws, under the guidance of Infinite wisdom.

Everything that exists is necessary.

Nature, the off-spring and product of the
Great First Cause, contains within itself the
essential substances and properties necessary
for the formation of matter.

Every part of nature is in harmony with
every other part. All nature is in harmony
with God its author.

Now if we can comprehend a great Ocean of
Light emanating from the Grand Centre containing within it Life, Law, Order, Cause, Effect
and Purpose we need go no further. Outside
of this all is myth.

CHAPTER II.

Fourth. The great centre of all things being spiritual, all power is necessarily spiritual.

Power is pressure acting through space. We can think of no definition more appropriate, whether applied in a physical, mental or moral sense.

We cannot manufacture power out of nothing, any more than space or matter.

Coal and other combustible matter used for the purpose contain the power imparted to them by the Sun ages before; we merely liberate that power pent up in the material consumed to procure it.

The law of the conservation of force teaches that power once in being can never cease to exist.

Science has given no definite answer to the question " What is the origin of power ?" Science is an investigator into the nature of *effects ;* it requires philosophy to understand the nature of *cause.*

Science will tell you, " the origin of power," as a general thing, " is heat." In its operation upon matter the student will see the force it possesses in the expansion of bodies, and in separating the particles from each other. This, however, is merely superficial.

Heat, and its apparent opposite, cold, are the results produced by certain vibrations of matter, differing in degree. The cause of these vibrations is a combination of different forces.

The *positive* and the *negative* united form the condition of existence.

God is the GREAT POSITIVE. Nature proceeding from Him by virtue of His creative energy is *negative*. The thing created can have no power, except what is imparted to it by the Creator.

All one can see of nature is matter in the multitudinous shapes it assumes. It is brought into form by the operation of invisible spiritual force. Natural law. We use the word spirit in contradistinction to matter.

Spirit is associated with the idea of life, energy, force, motion. Matter has none of these.

The different forms of matter are produced by the combination of different forces operating at different rates of motion.

There is no power in matter *per se*, for the chemist will take the hardest substance, and by the application of heat, so disturb the cohesive forces of the atoms of which different bodies are constituted, that in a short time it

will become dilated, reduced to a fluid, and then
to an invisible gas. This is the result of a law
of nature, that is, a law proceeding from the
source of all power operating upon matter. The
heat itself becoming less particled, rarified, sub-
limated and refined passes into its ultimate, Elec-
tricity. The latter being that subtle, elastic,
invisible substance which pervades all things,
and enters into every avenue between the finest
particles of matter.

Thus the lower evidences of power containing
and developing the higher, and the higher again
acting on all below its elevated state of perfection.

Motion, the result of power, is co-existent
with matter. There can be no expression of
motion without matter or the reverse. They necessarily exist together and are the off-spring
of power. God being the Great Centre of all
things. Nature being *passive* all power and
energy proceeds from Him—the Great Spirit
—and is Spiritual.

CHAPTER III.

Fifth. That man, being the highest order of organized intelligence, has a spiritual nature as well as a corporeal ; the spiritual having an organized form, with parts and organs corresponding to those of the visible body.

S xth. That the body being but matter, is formed as a covering for the spirit by the operation of natural law in accordance with the requirements and necessities of each individual for a use, serves its purpose, and then by operation of the same law, disintegrates and fades away. The living organized spiritual being remains and is immortal, having continued mental and moral growth.

God the Great Spirit fills with Life and Light the whole universe.

Life being everywhere, requires only the presence of necessary conditions and circumstances, for its organization into individualized existence possessing the elements of both a spirit body and a material body—a spiritual nature as well as a corporeal, assuming a form that can never change its essential constitution, or the laws of its nature, preserving its identity through all time, growing in spirit, and becoming developed in form, as the requirements of its nature draw to it the particles of matter necessary for its maturity.

The arrangement and process for man's spiritual, mental and material organization and development, are like all nature's laws, perfect in the powers, resources and capabilities, necessary for his growth and structure.

During this process of growth the spirit never loses its affinity for the spirit world; and the material form or outward body its affinity for the material world.

As the spirit part grows in stature and mental development, by the operation of a beautiful natural law, it is gradually covered with the materialized form, corresponding to all its requirements, wants and necessities, until it arrives at manhood, filling its designated place in God's great family.

During this process of growth and development, it experiences the operation and effect of those chemical laws which necessarily belong to the earth life. The sufferings of mind and body momentarily experienced, are part of the law of its nature, accompanying it while associated with materiality.

So intimately blended are the two, body and spirit, that one is created to grow and expand with the other, and, should premature dissolution take place, the spirit con-

tinues to grow and expand, assuming the
characters in the spirit world that the full
grown man would have occupied on earth.

When it arrives at mature manhood (in the
absence of premature dissolution) the work
of disintegration commences, and continues until the spirit no longer requires the material
covering; when, in obedience to the same law
of its nature, the companions before so intimately connected, separate forever, the material part going back to the great store-house
of particles, from which it was taken; the
spirit assuming its place in the new field of
existence, continues in the grand march of
mental, moral and spiritual development, to
an extent the mind, while associated with
earth, cannot comprehend.

CHAPTER IV.

Seventh. That there is a spiritual world, a place of existence for man after he has become separated from the form, with its substantial realities, adapted to the wants and necessities of his continued existence. That the change called physical death, a separation of matter and spirit, is a necessity of his nature quite as much as his birth, and does not essentially change the mental condition or other characteristics of any when experienced.

Eighth. That after the process of physical death the condition of the man in the spirit world depends not upon arbitrary decree or special provision made by a superior, but on character, aspirations and personal individual conformity to the universal divine law of his nature.

The two parts of man's nature, the spiritual and material, nothwithstanding their close relationship, keep up and maintain their distinctive affinities for the worlds to which their respective natures belong.

Of a two-fold nature all men are entirely conscious. They know that the body will die and return to its natural element, the earth. And there are but few, if any, who have not an innate conception of a future state of existence. However much they may differ in opinion as to its nature, all agree that life is continuous. That the spirtual is everlasting. The mind, unless laboring under an imperfect condition, cannot depart from the idea of spirit perpetuity, no more than it can recede from the knowledge that the body must die.

Man, therefore, is not ignorant of his two distinct natures, experiencing daily the natural decay of the body, and the continuous development of the great fact that his spirit is eternal. It requires no *Revelation* to teach these things, for it is a law of nature with which man becomes quite as familiar as with any other feature of his existence.

Indeed it would appear unnatural had man been brought into existence without this knowledge.

Man needs no evidence but a knowledge of his own nature to prove *Immortality*.

Now if the spirit lives forever, which all, or nearly all, are ready to admit, there must be a spirit-world in which it can reside, with substantial realities adapted to its nature and wants. This requires no argument. If the spirit lives it must have a place wherein it can exist, and it is reasonable to suppose that after leaving the body, by the natural law of affinity, it will be conducted to a locality adapted to its condition and capacity.

After the death of the body the spirit has a loftier aspiration for the good, the true, and the beautiful. A stronger desire to acquire greater knowledge of itself and surroundings. It is in compliance with this law that we suppose localities to exist in which the attributes, desires and characteristics of the spirit may be rapidly and distinctly developed.

The beautiful laws of nature, like their Divine Author, are just and equal in their effects, and it would be incompatible with the idea of justice, to suppose that a pure spirit would be kept daily and hourly in contact with other spirits whose minds and acts were entirely opposed to its own. This would be a violation of the natural law of PROGRESSION.

The following extract from a communication said to have been received by a very intelligent spiritualist (Judge Edmunds), is about as natural a description of the spirit-world as we have seen.

The reader will remember the proposition "that the change called physical death, a separation of matter and spirit, is a necessity of man's nature quite as much as his birth." Both are natural.

" When awakening from this sleep of death

and opening his eyes to the world into which his spirit was ushered, how strange his thoughts, how marvellous the sensations which rush through his brain with lightning rapidity! To you, who have some conception of spirit life, the ideas I have suggested will not appear so passing strange. The spirit-bond which connected it to matter is severed, the link of life is broken, the spirit freed is disengaging itself from its earthly trammels. There lies the body stretched in death. How unlike the spirit which is floating over it, unconscious, still unable to think, but just borne into the life of the spheres. As it floats over the body which was so lately its abiding place, there comes to it, drawn by their affection or by their duties, spirits possessing form and shape, beautiful beyond thought. They support this spirit-child until it recovers its consciousness, and then with the impress of the last life-thought still vibrating on its brain, with the emotions of its heart still unsubdued by death, with its whole nature palpitating, and even suffering at the thought of the separation from loved, aye! fondly loved friends, wife or children, this new spirit meets the new impressions and scenes which surround it. Its agonized mind writhing with death, and with all its nature struggling within its internal, it opens its eyes to the unspeakable glories of

a new world. Then all the spirits whose lives
are pure, whose mission being accomplished
toward it, now take it by the hand, and bid
it look around, and behold the things which
are old become new. Think you, with all these
objects, both of spirit-life and spirit-matter,
coursing their way through the several senses
of its brain, there is not awakened an impulse
and desire far beyond the dull and confined
sensations of life? Think, too, that it is dives-
ted of all the contrivances which in life so cir-
cumscribed its mental action, and that its freed
spirit can now quaff deep of the intoxicating
draughts of joy unspeakable that are presented
to it on all sides.

Spirits when they awake to a sense of what
they are, are not permitted to talk much,
neither are their minds tasked with a succes-
sion of new impressions other than those
which first meet the eye. After the friends
have taken charge of them for awhile, they
remain under their teaching for a time, not
sermons or doctrines, but a sort of history
of what is before them, and then they are
left to the true manifestations of their nature. Now, if good and pure, if their minds
desire the high and holy, if, in simple lan-
guage, they wish to ascend, their affinities are
their guide. They cannot mistake. They are

irresistibly impelled to go forward to the place where they meet with all the circumstances and conditions which conform to their desires or the wants of their nature.

Now, be it understood, spirits cannot conceal their true feelings like man. The fact of being a spirit opens the avenues of thought and motive to all. Thus, though their desires are as different and as varied as their forms and countenances, yet they are fully cognizant of what spirit means and of what spirit requires. It is this principle which impels them to locate where they will be most happy."

CHAPTER V.

Ninth. That growth and development is the law of
the human being, and is the endless progressive
destiny of all.

Tenth. That as individuals are continually passing
from the earthly to the spirit world, in all stages
and conditions of mental and moral growth, the
spirit world necessarily includes all grades of
character, from the lowest to the highest.

Eleventh. That happiness and misery depend on the
growth and development of moral purity, and
there must be as many grades of each in the
spirit world as there are shades of character,
each gravitating to its own place by the natural
law of affinity.

That growth and development is the law of
the human being, can scarcely admit of a doubt,
to the mind of even moderate comprehension.
We see the *principle* demonstrated in a material way even in the vegetable kingdom.

The tendency of the mind of man, is to
investigate and explore nature's laws. We
can scarcely conceive of a mind entirely des-
titute of an inclination to acquire knowledge.
Experience being the great educator, every
person must from necessity become more and

more acquainted with the physical manifestations of nature, and, as knowledge is acquired,
the mind becomes enlarged and rises into
lofty aspirations, wishes and desires.

There is no mind so enlightened, but there
is one above it, more developed, more pro-
gressed. Thus all advanced minds have above
them others still more advanced. At the
present day there are more persons moving
and controlling the affairs of life ; and
they are further advanced in a knowledge of
physical sciences, mental and moral development, grand spiritual truths, and manifest
more of the true characteristics of the proper
nature of humanity, than all nations or peoples who have preceded them.

" There is a necessity for an advance toward
perfection in everything created by God. Of
what purpose was it that he created worlds,
and filled them with intelligent beings, capable of understanding and learning from every
manifestation of his power around them the
effects, which certain laws he has established
have produced ? Of what purpose was it
that he should have created them, if he
had intended that they—man or men—should
have remained in a state of abeyance ? Of
what use the mind ? Of what use thought ?
Of what use that the sprig should have been
lopped from the oak itself ?

God could just as well have created man
without a soul as with an intelligent one; and
certainly it appears reasonable that in planting
within his body a spirit susceptible, comprehensive and intelligent, he intended that spirit
should not be satisfied with learning or understanding one fact only, and that it should not
be satisfied till it had grasped everything
within the scope of its faculties. If it were
not intended that both spirit and matter
should progress, God would probably have
created man with all the powers and faculties
of his nature, ready developed at his creation.
For, were it denied that the intention of his
creation was his steady advancement, the mind,
when it had mastered one position, would have
still remained the same as before it recognized
a new idea. There could not have been any
appreciation of anything before it, and instead
of knowledge enlarging its range of desire
and thought, it would have left it in the same
condition as it found it."

All grades of mind and character, from the
imbecile to the highest order of intellect; from
the most depraved and undeveloped in a mental and moral sense, to the most pure and
elevated, are momentarily passing from this
plane of existence to the spirit-world. That
world necessarily includes all grades of character.

" Life in the spirit world is but a continua-
tion of life upon earth, and that the legitimate
object of the one is but to prepare for the
other; that time on earth is but a stepping-
stone to an eternity in the spheres ; that the
bias and direction of the mind, and the affec-
tions which it obtains on earth, make their impress upon your existence after you have left
it; that the perversions and misdirections
which you imbibe during your primary existence affect and direct your life after it ; that
the truths which are planted in the soul while
it inhabits its tenement of clay, accompany
and cheer it on its way through the long ages
of eternity."
*   *   *   *   *   *   *   *   *

" To ascertain what was the true mission of
Christ, we should attentively consider the
character of the man as given in sacred history, and also in profane, and view his daily
life and action in reference to the great work
he was called to perform. The earliest indica-
tion of any positive ministration was his teachings in the temple when yet a child, and when
he confounded the Priest and the Pharisee.
At this time he reasoned of life, death, and
eternity, and the ground-work of all his teachings was, that the moral purity of man's life
on earth was the guarantee of his happiness
after death. From this period until the time

of his death he sought out every opportunity
to utter those sentiments; and were we to
take the sermon on the Mount as the solitary
evidence in support of our argument, we
should triumphantly claim that Christ's mission was the reformation of the moral condition of the world; that he taught that love,
purity, truth on earth, are the incipient steps
of progression; that eternity develops no sentiments more consonant with the nature of
God than progression from these principles.
The simple parable of the Pharisee and the
sinner is pertinent proof of the truth. The
Pharisee, satisfied with himself, desired no advance, but thanked God he was not like other
men; but the sinner, conscious of his short-
comings, convicted of sin, and of righteous-
ness, and of a judgment to come, besought
God to be merciful, to open to his mind the
truths it behooved him to know, and to assist
him in his earnest endeavors to progress in
all goodness from life through death, onward
through the spheres. What other interpreta-
tion can be given of this simple story related
by Christ? The sinner lifting up his eyes
afar off, cried, God be merciful! Merciful for
what? That he might understand how to
live, that his death might usher him into the
liberty of life everlasting."—(*Spiritualism.*)

CHAPTER VI.

Twelfth. That through the law of spirtual affinity there may be, and, doubtless are, by mental impression or other modes of transmission, communications to a limited extent from spirits out of the form to spirits in the form ; but these communications are to be regarded as truths, just as communications from one person to another while on earth. Their character for truthfulness depends entirely upon the mental and moral development of both—the one that gives and the one that receives.

Thirteenth. That these communications or influx of ideas and promptings from the spirit world are not to be regarded as special privileges, confined to one class of persons, but have existed and will exist through all time and among all classes ; they are the op.ration of natural law.

In the whole range of science, philosophy and theology, there is no one thing so interesting, in fact, all absorbing, as man's future *destiny.* Let there appear but one ray of light penetrating the future, and from the least developed to the towering intellect, silent, solemn attention is given. All else for the moment sinks into utter insignificance.

The great problems " Where are we from ? "

" Who are we ?" and " where are we going"?
have not yet been fully solved. If we should
remain in comparative ignorance of the first
and second, the third will ever be to those on
earth, the same intensely interesting question.

Is it a fact that those who have passed
through the process of physical death and are
in a spiritual state of existence, able by
mental impression, physical manifestations or
otherwise, to transmit their thoughts, wishes
and desires to those who are yet connected
with the material body, and if so under what
conditions, and to what extent? are questions
now claiming more attention and consideration
than any other thing.

The immortality of the soul, or continued
existence of the spirit of man, may be con-
sidered as settled in the minds of all. Few,
if any, really doubt it.

While each person has a distinct individualized organization, no two among the countless
numbers existing at any one time are pre-
cisely alike.

There is such a similarity in mental organization, thought, feeling, aspiration, will,
wish and desire, that were it not for the
difference in the physical organization, it
would be often almost impossible to tell one
from the other.

These thoughts, likes and desires appear to run in the same groove. This is what philosophers call " *affinity.*"

Is it unreasonable to suppose that these persons when separated by the very thin partition which is said to divide the spiritual from the natural world still have an inclination to commune with each other, so far as their different conditions of existence would permit? Particularly when they had been closely allied while both were in the physical form, by love, marriage or other relationship?

Matter, Mind and Spirit are the three principles constituting organized individuality.

Matter we can see and feel, because it has form. We associate Spirit with form also, but Mind we cannot comprehend. It is the agent or vehicle by which communications and thought are transmitted from spirit to spirit. There is no other conceivable way.

The different proportions of Matter, Mind and Spirit, constitute the different dispositions, powers, capacities, &c., of individuals.

It is a well established fact, generally received as such, that there are persons (clairvoyants) at times possessing a power to discern objects not generally perceptible to the senses of themselves or others, and while in that condition, their minds are greatly developed and made cognizant of principles and truths, pertaining not only to the physical condition of things, but their relationship to the higher and more exalted state of existence.

Persons of extraordinary capacities and abilities, are endowed, more or less, with this power. Grand and beautiful truths are discovered while in this condition. In fact, the ability for which persons are often distinguished is altogether owing to the fact of their possessing it.

While in this developed state of mind, spirit out of the body, undoubtedly acts upon spirit in the body, producing results inexplicable in any other way. That is, an impression is made by the spirit in a more exalted condition, on the inner principle of the spirit receiving it. The impression creates thought, which thought becomes associated with words, and are thus communicated to others.

These impressions find vent in different ways, depending upon the peculiar organization of the medium. Their character for usefulness and truthfulness depend entirely upon the mental and moral development of the one that gives and the one that receives.

All persons possess mediumistic powers to a greater or less extent. They are not confined to a select few. Many are unconscious of their existence in themselves. They develop themselves in various ways, scarcely two being alike.

Various theories have been given of the *modus operandi* of Spirit communication, but no one really understands or can explain the means used. The law of spirit affinity is exceedingly mysterious. We see its operations and effects daily among and between the sexes, but cannot tell the cause of its existence. Upon it, however, depends the little harmony that exists among men.

Whether a spirit out of the body can return to the earth, draw from the elements matter to cover itself with a body similar to the one it used while in the form, with all its organs, parts and acquirements, use it as long as it wishes, and then withdraw, allowing it to almost instantly disappear and return to the source from which it came, is *more than doubtful*. In fact, it appears to be *wholly inconsistent with the laws of nature.*

CHAPTER VII.

Those who have given spirit-materialization some attention, claim that spirits become possessed of such an extensive knowledge and control of the laws of chemical affinity, that they are enabled to decompose and recompose solid bodies of matter, to suspend the force of cohesion, so that the particles will be for a time set free, and when they withdraw that suspension the same particles will immediately assume their former positions and relationship to each other, the body of matter returning to its exact form and shape before decomposition took place.

By this means, also, they are enabled to remove heavy bodies from one place to another. They suspend the force of cohesion, the particles of matter become disconnected, the spirits then move the *spirit* of the body to the desired place, the scattered particles follow, and with unerring certainty and precision again assume their respective places.

That spirits possess such power is highly improbable. If such were the case, the forms of matter would be, to say the least, in a very unsettled, if not *unsafe* condition.

That nature's laws can be suspended, and held in abeyance by spirits to such a formidable extent, needs confirmation from very high authority.

Clairvoyants undoubtedly can *see* spirits, but they are not *materialized;* and wherever in sacred or profane history mention is made of angels and spirits having been *seen*, if not wholly imaginary, it was by persons in a *clairvoyant* condition. The following is part of a communication purporting to come from a spirit describing the process of materialization.

"In order that a spirit may present itself in what is understood as a materialized form, so as to be seen by your external visual organs, they must have their spiritual bodies covered, more or less densely, with a tangible material substance. The material substance is not drawn from your physical bodies, nor from the atmosphere, but the forces which produce it are drawn from the medium, the circle, and the atmosphere.

We do not take your skin, nor your flesh and blood, to create these material forms, but we take the forces which produce these tissues in part from you. It is usual, in the first place, presenting a materialized form of a spirit, simply to cover the exterior of the body with the materials thus formed, so that you

have little more than what the artist terms
" still life," in these. We have the power,
however, of materializing the internal organs;
especially the organs of speech, so that spirits
are able to give utterance to vocal sounds.

We can also materialize the *spiritual heart*,
blood vessels, and all *the other organs*, so that
you may *feel* the *pulse* and become cognizant
of their existence.

*   *   *   *   *   *   *

This is in artistic work, requiring a knowledge of the laws by which it is performed, as
well as a skill which can only be obtained by
repeated practice. Materialization produced by
different spirits will vary. There are numerous schools here in which this art is taught;
pupils are trained and sent out to practice."

There are said to be many phases of mediumship; this opens such a wide field for
credulity, delusion and deception, that it is
often almost impossible to tell the genuine
from the spurious. There are a few general
rules, however, if closely observed by investi-
gators, deception can be detected:

First. Very few mediums who follow the ex-
hibition of spirit manifestations as a *business*,
are reliable. They generally consult the will
and wishes of those who patronize them. Every

honest investigator will acknowledge this to be true.

Second. When mediums are scrupulously exacting about certain arbitrary ◦ "*conditions*" to be observed by the circle, it is not a favorable sign of honesty.

Third. When *darkness* and *music* are required for the display of spirit-manifestations, the investigator may feel assured that imposition is about to be practised.

Fourth. When spirits refuse in any way to identify themselves, give evasive answers to plain questions, or, the communications they give are shrouded in mystery, it is very seldom that the medium is not an impostor.

That denizens of the spirit-world do communicate by mental impression or other modes of transmission, with the spirits of persons who are yet in the material form, is a fact, so well established, no one whose opinion would be regarded as of any value, can successfully deny. But it is equally true that where there is one genuine communication four are spurious. Those that are genuine contain nearly all grades of character. Nevertheless after twenty years' experience, the writer can truthfully say, that he never saw a *genuine* communication contain a word or sentence that was *immoral.*

Education in the spirit-world, as it is here, is

slow of growth. The illiterate, undeveloped
spirit, on its first entrance into that world, experiences but little change in its condition.

The following communications believed to be
genuine, received by a friend, is a specimen of
the intellectual condition of one who had been
in the spirit-world but a few months. It is
given as written. He said his name was "John
Jones," had "died in New York, in January,"
1862. The communication was received in May
of the same year.

"You have got to hear my story fust. I am
happy now since I have larnt how fer to wrap.
You must pitty my ignorence instead of laugh-
ing. I can tell you, I am sorry I lived as I
did; but no decent man would speak to me
when I wanted to reform, and now I am not
able to converse as well as a little infant, because I have no body to larn me how. Now
do remember the poor; and remember that
poverty makes 'em bad. You must not pass
them by. I lived anywhere where they would
keep me. Good-night, Sur."

Through the mediumship of Mrs. Nellie J.
T. Brigham, well known to the public, we have
listened to many most beautiful and sublime
productions of literature. Among other things,
she will improvise poetry upon any subject

selected for her by entire strangers, without a moment's preparation.

On one occasion when the writer was present, she asked for a suitable subject for a Poem; there was handed her a slip of paper, upon which was written "The Water Lily." Without hesitation, delay, or apparent effort on her part, she delivered in a clear, distinct voice, the following beautiful Poem:

" Dark beneath the skies of winter,
   Lies the sluggish water low,
While the sombre clouds above it,
   Drifting masses come and go ;
And beneath the silent water
   Lies a germ that is at rest,
Waiting neath the slime and darkness
   While hope whispers in its breast.

Soon the ice of weary winter
   Melts and passes all away,
And unfolding buds and blossoms
   Pave the fragrant path of May ;
And the golden sunbeams quiver
   On the river shining through,
Telling all the happy story,
   "Earth is fair and skies are blue."

Calling, "Oh ! thou child of Heaven
   Light is given for thy way—
Rise ! the winter has departed,
   Night has passed, lo it is day."

Then the listning lily rises,
  Climbing upward to the light,
Till amid the leaves encircling
  Comes the blossom into sight.

Whence comes all the wealth of whiteness,
  And the beauty of the snow,
With its heart of golden glory,
  Where the treasured sunbeams glow ;
From the dark and silent waters,
  From the ooze and mud below,
It arose with patient toiling,
  Till God clothed it white as snow.

So in all your grief and doubting,
  In this winter world of sin,
Take the lesson of the lilies,
  All your weary hearts within.
Hope through all your nights of sorrow,
  For a morrow bright and fair,
Where the soul is lifted upward
  From the waters of despair.

Rise though sorrow's waves are bitter ;
  Rise. from darkness and from wrong,
Thou shalt find the smile of Heaven
  And thy soul shall bloom ere long,
And within the land of beauty,
  Thou shalt find rejoicing there,
Blooming like the *water lily*
  From all earthly grief and care."

Mrs. B. in her normal condition makes no

pretentions to literary attainments or poetical ability.

This is a common occurrence among public lecturers on the Spiritualistic Rostrum, but this circumstance is related, because it occurred in the writer's presence.

Whoever has listened to the unsurpassed eloquence of Miss Jennie Leys while she was under an influence, must have felt satisfied that there was an intelligence present, far surpassing hers while in a normal condition.

Those who have been in the spirit-world a long time have probably lost all interest in earthly affairs. Their high mental and moral attainments being so far above the comprehension of mortals yet in the flesh, that it would be useless for them to communicate. They could not be understood.

CHAPTER VIII.

Fourteenth. That the chain of causation traced backward from what we see in nature, leads inevitably to a Great First Cause, the fountain of life, love and wisdom, the source of all power, sustaining to all individualized intelligence the relation of *father*, consequently all are *brethren.*

Does nature furnish evidence sufficient to prove the existence of a Great First Cause?

Every well balanced, properly organized human mind must answer this question in the affirmative.

We can only recognize Power, Intelligence, Wisdom, Mind, by signs, results, consequences.

We can see the little seed placed in the ground, and from it will grow a huge tree, bearing fruit which contains within it hundreds of seeds of the same kind, any one of which embraces the proper elements to produce another tree. The same principle runs through the animal kingdom. We see the result in the multitudinous forms of matter, but we cannot see the power or individual law, the operation of which produces these numerous forms. We know from observation that every blade of grass,

every shrub, every tree, and every animal has
a distinctive law of its nature, and these various laws work in harmony with all other laws
in the economy of nature, all coming from
the same power, and the various producing,
generating, organizing forces having one common origin. In all their operations, there is
method, order, purpose, result. Philosophy can
come to but one conclusion, Reason give but
one solution, summed up in a few words—ALL
NATURE'S FORMS IN THE MINERAL, VEGETABLE
AND ANIMAL KINGDOMS ARE BUT THE DEMON-
STRATIONS OF ONE GRAND POWER, A VITAL
FORCE, OF INFINITE EXTENT AND DURATION,
POSSESSING INTELLIGENCE, MIND, PURPOSE, RE-
SULT.

This Power is the Life, the Soul, the Spirit
of matter.

This Spirit is OUR GOD.

Each form in the Mineral and Vegetable
kingdoms, and each organized Intelligence having an existence in the animal, being the result
of the operation of a separate law, has its appropriate place in Nature's Great Structure, the
smallest as proportionately important as the
largest.

Nature makes no distinction in the operation
of her laws; in the distribution of her favors she
has no preference. The sun shines upon all

alike. The gentle showers of rain refresh the
little rose in the desert as well and as cheerfully
as the one in the garden.

For the human family nature provides no law
entailing upon one class rights, privileges and
immunities more than upon others. All men are
created equal, and have natural, moral, political
and social rights; the social relations being
regulated by the laws of congeniality or affinity.

Whenever mention is made in sacred or profane history of a portion of any nation, tribe or
kingdom, having been set apart for any particular purpose, or where they have assumed a position in society by which they obtained legal or
ecclesiastical rights, privileges or exemptions,
greater than others, it is the history of a direct
and positive violation of the laws of God, as
manifested through nature.

Whenever any government in its sovereign
capacity grants special favors or exclusive privileges to any portion of its subjects, it is an arbitrary assumption and abuse of power which no
government has a right to exercise. It is usur-
pation and tyranny, always producing a retard-
ing and demoralizing influence on the people.

Wherever any sect or denomination throws
around itself barriers to exclude others who
might wish to partake of any advantages it may
have for mental, moral or social improvement,

without being obliged to submit to a particular form, or to believe in a certain creed or dogma, assumes a position in society, selfish, unwise, unnatural and unjust to all others of the same community, state or nation.

The Great First Cause which we call God, being the source of all power, from which power proceeds laws that in their operation produce the different forms in nature, constituting the mineral, vegetable and animal kingdoms, these laws working in harmony, producing proper and intended results with unerring certainty; man being the ultimatum of all organized intelligence, and being as subject to the law of his nature as any other material form, and these laws all being controlled by Divine wisdom, constitute all men *brethren*, standing upon equal terms of relationship with the *Great Father*.

4

CHAPTER IX.

Fifteenth. That man as the offspring of the Divine, has within him a germ of divinity, which is ever prompting him toward perfection, and that all evil in man is a want of harmony with this Divine principle, caused by an undeveloped mental and moral condition.

Man has a natural body consisting of gross matter, and a spiritual body consisting of organized matter, in a state of refined advancement. He has two natures, a material and a spiritual. The material limited in its duration. The spiritual contains within it the ESSENCE, the Mind, the Intelligence, the Life, the *Immortal Man*, with perpetual, eternal, everlasting existence.

There is in man a principle which is stronger than Reason. An activity, a Sovereign Energy, conscious of its own power, independence and duration. It thinks, it feels, it has judgment, it reasons. It has an innate perception that it will live forever, that it will ultimately arrive at a condition of perfection. It is above the undeveloped part of man's nature, all the other faculties consent to the propriety and necessity of obedience to this power.

Dr. Adam Clark calls this feature of man's

organization "*the will*," and comments on it thus:—"There is not a man in ten millions, who will carefully watch the operations of this faculty, that will find it opposed to good, and obstinately attached to evil, as is generally supposed. Nay, it is found almost uniformly on God's side, while the whole sensual system is against Him. It is not the WILL that leads men astray; but the corrupt PASSIONS which oppose and oppress the *will.* It is truly astonishing into what endless mistakes men have fallen on this point, and what systems of divinity have been builded on these mistakes. The will, this almost only friend to God in the human soul, has been slandered as God's *worst enemy.*"

This is but illustrating under the name of the *will,* the germ of divinity that is in man. It cannot do evil, but, on the contrary, is ever prompting man to a higher, holier and happier condition.

Just in proportion to the development of man's mental and moral faculties, will be the condition of his passions. Good and evil are but names for opposite conditions. As he develops the latter recedes, and the former increases; still advancing toward perfection. Thus, man is ever *progressing,* and this is the law of his nature.

CHAPTER X.

Sixteenth. That growth in goodness and truth is slow,
depending to some extent on physical organization and surrounding circumstances, but the ultimate destiny of all is perfection and happiness.

Seventeenth. Man's highest duty in this world is to
assist in the mental and spiritual development of
his kind, for such is the fundamental unity of
human interests. So completely are our essential
lives merged in each other's, that the highest good
and happiness of each individual can only be at-
tained through the highest good and happiness of
all.

All men grow in goodness and truth. Man's
spiritual nature can never degenerate. Matter decomposes and changes in form, but never
grows less in quantity or value. The spirit
having within it life eternal, from the necessities of its nature, continually increases in
knowledge and wisdom, advances in goodness
and truth. The physical organization of men
often retard their progress. The position they
occupy in life may be such as to prevent an
accumulation of the elements necessary for
their rapid mental and moral development,
but the growth is sure, the ultimate destiny

certain. Perfection and happiness is the final
condition of every child of God.

In very early life man is taught the pri
mary lessons of God's great administration, as
manifested through the laws of nature.

The little child at first has no knowledge
but its own wants. It feels its own necessities,
and is eager to have them supplied; and not
until it comes in contact with others of its
own age, does it learn that they have wants
as well as itself. Its little selfish nature
prompts it to gratify its own wishes first, and
even then it gives with reluctance to others.
Not until it has advanced from childhood to
youth, does it realize that it derives pleasure
in bestowing upon its comrades that assist-
ance which gratifies its own wishes.

Advancing to manhood, the love of wealth,
the commanding influence it gives in the
world, the fascinations of power, and the
gratification of distinction in life, to a great
extent obscures the finer sensibilities of man's
nature. It is not until the cares and troubles,
the vexations and sorrows, trials and disappointments of life are experienced, and keenly
felt; until the cold winds and nipping frosts of
life's autumn have softened and subdued the
uncouth, selfish and baser passions of his
nature, does man realize the great fact, that

human lives and human interests, through infinite wisdom, are so united and merged in each other, that each individual can only attain to a high condition of goodness and happiness by others occupying the same position. Some will probably never be able to realize it in this world, regardless of age or experience.

When man has advanced to this standpoint, and not until then, will be seen towering above and completely transcending all other conceptions, the beautiful Tree of Life in all its symmetrical glory, the roots firmly fixed in nature, its growth having been promoted by the fertilizing influence of charity, love, justice and the performance of good actions; its blossoms transmitting through all humanity an exhilarating fragrance of affection and kindly greeting, binding the interests, feelings and associations of men into one common brotherhood; its branches speading over all peoples, powers and principalities, " its leaves for the healing of all nations."

CHAPTER XI.

Eighteenth. The sufferings of this life are the necessary results of man's structure, are essential conditions of his mental, moral and spiritual culture
and development; they are part of the divine
economy, and the only methods by which we can
ever reach high attainments and beneficent results.
No man can appreciate spiritual refinement and
exaltation, or comprehend the full measure of happiness and joy, until he has felt the sharp pangs of
suffering and woe.

Nineteenth. That in proportion to man's *moral
purity* will be his happiness here and hereafter.

The elements of which the human body are
composed are found to exist in nearly all
animal bodies. In fact, it is only the propor-
tionate difference of the same elements, the
characteristics of the mind, passion and purpose they are required to develop, represent,
and for which they are intended, that govern
the formation of the physical structure of all
animals.

The mind becomes lost when attempting to
compute the time it required nature to prepare
the material elements which enter into the
structure of the animal kingdom before the

different formations were prepared to receive
that living, thinking, reasoning, organized existence, germ of the Divinity, which gives per-
putuity to man's duration, if not to inferior
animals. These great constructive processes
are correspondingly destructive; the results of
the operation of a law marching on in effect
with methodical precision, the commencement
and duration incomprehensible to the human
mind.

The laws of cohesion and disintegration
never cease in their operation; the first only
preparatory for the last. Nature is never at
rest. All these apparent differences, tumults and
commotions, are but necessary parts of the
grand whole, in perfect harmony with each
other, and with the plans and purposes of the
Great First Cause, the Divine Origin.

Nature's forms being but temporary struc-
tures, serving for incidental purposes, whenever the ends for which they were made are
accomplished, disintegrate and pass off into
other uses, proceeding with mathematical ex-
actness. A place for everything, and everything in its place. Nothing comes too soon,
nothing delays.

It has been said that the agitations and
commotions of the material world are "caused
by nature seeking an equilibrium." A great

fallacy. Nature is in exact equilibrium. There is nothing out of order. No mistakes are or ever will be made.

The infinite is God. The *nearest* the infinite is man.

We accept the idea that Man is the Ultimate of Nature, the Lord of Creation, and that his destiny is a perfectly formed spiritual body, a symmetrically developed mind, occupying an exalted spiritual position ,capable of enjoying perfect happiness, and that this condition is to be obtained by means of outward agents, the operation of natural laws for spiritual advancement.

Man, before he is capable of enjoying an exclusively spiritual existence, must be educated, unfolded, cultured, developed, until he is made conscious of his spiritual destiny and relationship with divine things. He can only be educated through experience, and for that purpose, the law of his nature requires a primary. existence in a material body, through which he can receive that culture and discipline that will prepare him for higher attainments. It is only by association with gross matter that he can learn the conditions of a lower existence, and then by these powerful agencies brought into use under the direction of Divine Intelligence, he gradually acquires a knowledge of the high purpose of his creation.

His education is compulsory. Rarely does
he consent to that thorough discipline so
necessary for his advancement. The following article, published in the Philadelphia
Ledger, in the issue of the 23d of August,
1873, will be read in this connection with interest. The author's name is not known, or
his permission to use it would have been
asked.

" There are few of us, if any, who are suf-
ficiently judicious and well balanced thoroughly to appreciate and value the steady
and unvarying discipline of nature. Because
we cannot always trace the immediate connection between actual wrong-doing and suffering,
we are frequently inclined to consider nature's
penalties stern and hard, if not arbitrary and
unjust. The pain she inflicts appears to us
to be often greatly out of proportion to the
faults that preceded it. We see not why the
accidental misstep should be visited by a
broken limb; why inherited disease should
produce lingering physical agony and premature death; why simple and perhaps unavoid-
able ignorance of the laws of nature should
entail such untold suffering and sorrow. Perhaps one reason why it is thus hard for us to
admit the constant friendliness of nature is
because we mistake the office of penalty. We
mix up with it some purpose of vengeance, or

at least an intention of inflicting a justly merited
and apportioned punishment for a direct offence, whereas the more closely we study
nature's laws the more we shall find their one
grand purpose to be the steady improvement
and elevation of the human race. Whatever
hinders or obstructs this, whether ignorance
or error, or moral defection, is continually being swept away, and the rude handling received is not so much in proportion to the actual moral guilt incurred, as to the degree of
obstruction offered to the progress of mankind. Viewed in this light, what seems to us
cruel in natural penalties, is really the largest,
wisest, kindest benevolence. In many cases
we can actually trace the workings of this
law. We know that the failure and poverty
of the idle, improvident or unskilful, however
painful to them to bear, are the means by
which patient industry and cultured labor are
developed; that the physical sufferings that
follow ignorance of nature's laws, are the
strongest incentives to the study of those
laws; that even the severity which sends to
an early grave the feeble and diseased off-
spring of unhealthy parents, or by an epi-
demic, weeds out so large a portion of the in-
temperate, vicious, and uncleanly, really puri-
fies the community and leads them into
improved conditions of life.

The farther we progress in knowledge the more we see and understand that the apparent cruelty of nature in her penalties is but the necessary means of working out a happiness real and permanent, because founded upon the eternal laws of being. If this be so, we may well trust nature where we cannot trace her, and believe that it is only because of our limited vision that we can ever deem her hard or unkind in any of her dealings. Could we thoroughly acquire this state of mind, it would counteract the tendency that is so common to interfere between cause and effect, and to dissociate ignorance and error from their natural penalties. Many of the reforms of the day, and much of the private beneficence of the world, loses its value from thus striving to prevent this natural sequence, and to save individuals from the results of their own conduct. The indulgence which surrounds the petted child of wealth with luxury, and shields him from every pain, is not real kindness, but cruelty. His powers, never tested, can never be developed; his faculties, unused, cannot wake into living action, and the only true happiness of man is that which comes from the full exercise of all his faculties. The indiscriminate charity which feeds idleness and nourishes vice, thus warding off for a time the penalties of both, is an actual injury both to the receiver and the community. All efforts to coerce men into good actions without establishing good principles, to restrict their freedom so that they cannot reap what they have sown; all flattery, insincerity and deceit; all excess of government; all measures which tend to reward ignorance, and put it on a par with wisdom and ability, are of this character. Instead of nature being cruel in visiting ignorance, error and misdoing with penalties, it is we who are cruel in striving to subvert her fidelity. It is, however, impossible to suspend nature's discipline long, if we could. There will ever be a reaction, and she will reassert her authority in spite of all our efforts to dispute it. Her laws are as inexorable as they are beneficent, and when we try to subvert them we are but beating against the waves.

It may be said, what room is there left for human benevolence? If nature's penalties are the best and surest means of human progress, and to avert them is but to hinder it, it might seem that no outlet was left through which we could help or benefit our fellow creatures. But this is not so. Every impulse of benevolence has a channel through which it may flow unimpeded to bless mankind. Not by divorcing folly from its fruits, not by interfering with natural results, or averting na-

tural penalties, can we do good, but rather by
making these results clear to the minds of
others, by endeavoring to dispel ignorance, en-
lighten error, and convince men of the inevita-
ble results of wrong doing. It is true this
work is difficult, while the other is easy; but
it is permanent, while the other is transient;
it strengthens the roots of character, while the
other spoils the bud by forcing it open. It is
comparatively easy to relieve the immediate
wants of a beggar, but to raise him from beg-
gary to self-support, to set before him the
degrading results of idleness, and the blessings
of honest industry, to excite within him better
aims, these are tasks at once difficult and
worthy of endeavor. To shield a criminal
from the consequences of his crime is at least
a questionable benevolence, but to convince
him of his wrong doing, and incite him to reform, is a noble enterprise. To guard a child
from evil is a small and negative work, but to
give him the power and the will to resist it is
a great and permanent blessing. It is in at-
tacking the roots of evil, not in warding off
its penalties; in dispelling error, not in averting the consequences; in instructing ignorance,
not in saving men from its effects, that true
benevolence, thus working with and not against
nature's kind and loving laws will accomplish
her mission of good to the world."

CHAPTER XII.

How thorough is man's discipline! How complete the means used for the purpose! How permanent and lasting his education!

All scientific knowledge; all facts necessary for the advancement and elevation of humanity; all great spiritual truths man has obtained through the means of danger, trials, difficulties, disappointments, blood, racks, gibbets, revolutions, convulsions, earthquakes, and other troubles and vexations incident to human nature, which are apt to be termed accidents, miracles, unnatural causes, &c., yet when understood and viewed from a proper stand-point display the wisdom and benevolence of the Deity as much as those called blessings.

"I come not to send peace, but a sword," said Christ.

"For I am come to set a man at variance against his father, and the daughter at variance against her mother, and the daughter-in-law against her mother-in-law."

This state of affairs always existed. There never has been a time when the human family lived in peace; there never was a time when

a single family dwelt together in perfect
harmony; kinsmen, friends and neighbors, never
lived on terms of friendship for any consider-
able length of time. The pretended fondness
of the two sexes for each other, is, to a very
great extent hypocrisy.

The great difference in likes and dislikes
that exist between man and wife, parents and
children, brothers and sisters, the want of congeniality between brothers, and between sisters,
is a fact transparent to all.

The duplicity, deceit, envy, hatred, malice,
back-biting and hypocrisy in every possible
phase, common among mankind, is part of his
nature.

No human laws can ever reform the drunk-
ard, debauchee, thief or the liar. They can be
punished by the force of statutory enactments,
but their dispositions can never thereby be
changed.

No moral reforms were ever brought about
by legislation, church discipline, or the en-
forcement of plenary decrees.

WHY does this condition of things exist?

We are living in the cellar kitchen. We are
in an undeveloped condition. The Planet is not
capable of producing a higher order of men.
These apparent deficiencies in the great human
family cannot be prevented; it is man's natural

condition. The tree can at present produce nothing but unripe fruit. The material world must reach maturity before it can produce the full grown man.

The supposed evils incident to this state of existence are not really enemies of humanity. If they were not necessary to our present condition they would not exist. "Life is but a battle and a march." These trials and difficulties are but gymnastic exercises, training us for a higher and more spiritual existence. They are the means by which we progress. Our failures in life are our successes. Our losses, our richest gains. Our greatest advances are over the ruins of cherished schemes.

The more we suffer in this world the faster we will progress in the next.

One of the attributes of the Divine Mind is Justice.

Whatever may be the difference in the organization of men, their condition in life, or their natural propensities, each one has to undergo the necessary discipline to qualify him for a higher life. Whatever may be the length of time required; whatever may be the condition we are in, or the surrounding circumstances; however rugged may be the paths we have to tread, or the apparent difficulties in our way, the great law of Jus-

tice demands no more from each one, and
will take no less than is exactly necessary to
qualify us for the purpose for which we are
intended.

For a wilful and malignant wrong against
a fellow-being, or for a direct and positive
violation of a law of one's nature, there is *no
forgiveness.* Nature's demands are inexorable;
they admit of no compromise; they will listen
to no reason; they will have the uttermost
farthing. For a departure from the laws of
eternal right, the penalty follows the trans-
gression to an extent commensurate with the
offence, and no more.

We must be perfected through suffering.
Justice accepts of nothing but compensation.
A *quid pro quo.*

CHAPTER XIII.

When in the course of events, mental, moral or social reform becomes necessary, or great changes in the condition of things are to take place, Divine wisdom, through nature, furnishes the proper persons and the necessary means for their accomplishment.

These persons are raised up generally from obscure places in society, but their organization and mental development, place them far in advance of the age in which they live. In this consists their superiority.

The world, not seeing as they see, knowing as they know, feeling as they feel, regard them as enthusiasts, mystical and visionary in their ideas, doctrines and theories. They are subjected to humiliation, repulsion, dislike and insult, sometimes to imprisonment, and even torture. The multitude is slow to learn, jealous of superiority, and with a superabundance of selfishness, envy and conceit, are loath to see others in advance of themselves.

The teachings and motives of these advanced persons are misunderstood, misinterpreted, and however much merit or intrinsic

value there may be in them, the ignorance
of the great mass may for a while retard
their progress.

But truth is powerful and will prevail. Just
as fast as the people are prepared for it,
they receive it, and although these persons
possessing great comprehensive minds, excel-
ling in wisdom and goodness may temporarily
suffer persecution at the hands of the ignorant and bigoted fanatics, their brilliant
thoughts will live, and throw light into the
dark corners of superstition, credulity and
ignorance, and their influence and excellence
will be transmitted down the current of time,
sending a thrill of delight, admiration and life
to thousands of kindred spirits ages thereafter.

The world must and will *progress*. It mat-
ters but little what name is given to progressive movements, they are the natural outflow
of a great, irresistible, spiritual power. The
life, the soul, the divine energy, operating
through natural laws, for uses, purposes, ends,
results, consequences; manipulating and controlling all organizations of mind and matter,
governments, kingdoms, systems and combina-
tions. The whole in minutiæ and detail, feels
the vitalizing, life-giving, developing effects,
invigorating and enlightening the intellectual
faculties, entering into the field of perception

and consciousness, promoting and advancing to a superior state of existence, enabling all eventually to comprehend from a philosophic and scientific stand-point, principles, causes, effects and their results; creating within the mind holier and more sublime aspirations, wishes and desires, for elevated and exalted spiritual attainments and conditions.

CHAPTER XIV.

Knowledge in former times was confined to a few. Now, on this Continent at least, by the aid of public schools and other modern facilities for acquiring information, the minds of the people have become stimulated to a high degree, and in all conditions of life may be found persons with thoughtful, well-informed, philosophical and even scientific attainments.

From the most unpretending to the giant intellect, the great subject which has most occupied the human mind, is "Immortality." Does man exist after life's fitful fever shall have been ended? If a man die, shall he live again? These are the great questions which have in the past, and will in the future ages of the world, overshadow all others.

The learning, the talent, the genius of the world have assembled to solve the great problem of man's genesis, object of life, and his destiny. The combat with superstition will doubtless be fearful, but the issue is by no means doubtful. Ignorance, credulity, bigotry, intolerance, religious fanaticism, and all enemies of truth, must give way and forever perish.

The fabulous stories which have been represented as "Revelations of the Divine will to man," have ceased to be regarded with the veneration our forefathers surrounded them. This is the age of *facts*, and facts are stubborn things. That system of religion or morals which will not stand the test of reason, should not be allowed to exist.

The battle in which Reason and Credulity are the contending parties, is being fought with great fury, but the contest will be of short duration. Never was there a combat between truth and error but the former was triumphant.

The spiritual part of man's nature demands a religion recognizing, a Common *Fatherhood* and a Common *Brotherhood*.

All opposition to this reasonable, but powerful demand, must eventually yield.

Caste has had its day, and will soon be numbered among the things of the past. The spirit of the present age is analytical, thorough, satisfied with nothing but what has truth for its foundation. It disregards the stronghold authority, and laughs at tradition. Its only standard is reason; it encourages the independence of the many, instead of recognizing the power of a few. It worships God through nature, by being obedient to nature's laws.

This is honoring the Diety, and is in harmony with his will.

The result of this mighty growth of mind
is *first*, to sweep away old errors; next, the
accumulation and arrangement of facts with
which to form a practical religion that will
develop and familiarize the human mind with
all the beautiful truths adapted to the wants
and necessities of man's nature while associated with materiality, and to cultivate within
him grander, higher and more noble aspirations for a future spiritual existence.

www.ingramcontent.com/pod-product-compliance
Lightning Source LLC
Chambersburg PA
CBHW022151090426
42742CB00010B/1461